Originally published June 24, 2018.

,,,

THE ANECDOTES

INCLUDING SOME INVOLVING INTELLECT, MYTHOLOGY, AND MODERN RELIGIONS

by Nathan Coppedge

,,,

INTRODUCTION

See also *100 Ideas on How to Get Rich.*

These quotations and stories were collected very informally beginning in the late 2010s. Some of them are owed in part to the Yale community, of which my dad was somewhat of a member since he attended Yale in order to complete his dissertation.

My own ties to Yale have not been as strong as I would like, though I was lucky enough to attend one course through an arrangement with top students during my final year in high school.

These stories are not all about Yale as much as I might like them to be. Instead, they draw on a more diverse fusion of themes from intellect and storytelling throughout the world.

I hope to add to the collection over the years as my memory seems to be becoming more strong with age.

,,,

Members of conspiracy believers network on reddit but how do you reach someone who considers every scientific paradigm suspect?

I'm not much of a reddit person, but no one seems to have answered your question, so I'll answer.

I'm actually not much of a conspiracy theorist, and the die-hard ones are hard to talk to in the extreme. Even if they were psychic I think you would have trouble getting straight information from them. They like to offend people, basically even if they have a developed personality. Some don't have much personality, then you run into "I just think" syndrome.

My own perspective is there are several different possible routes if we take the question more seriously which means in this case with a grain of salt:

(1) Possibly the person thinks UFO's are real, and it is hard to prove otherwise, and they generalize from that.

(2) Possibly secretly they like the feeling of the occult and supernatural. They have no reason to disbelieve in haunted houses.

(3) Possibly the person is 'going through experiences'. Maybe someone they know likes things related to Area 51 or the U.S. military, and they believe the military was connected with conspiracies, because conspiracies are

supposedly about government projects or something worse.

(4) Fourthly, someone may be investigating fringe science, and either believes fraudsters or has developed some level of scientific interest in an obscure field like the SETI Program or perpetual motion machines.

The first category is a bit naive, but they're probably right that extraterrestrials would be humanoid, and their thinking doesn't go much beyond that. The second category is sort of acceptable outside the Christian religion on the argument that millions of Christians believe in god, why not extend it to multiple gods, after all if magic exists someone could use it, and a lot of people believe miracles are possible if someone is lucky or if someone powerful intervenes. The third category is wrong and doesn't care. Because it's illegal to create a real conspiracy, fake conspiracies are okay. The fourth category doesn't mind being wrong part of the time, and this confuses other people. Maybe by SETI they don't expect alien life, but emotionally it's still an epic quest, which could turn up data of some kind. Maybe a habitable world. It could be baby steps. Same with perpetual motion. Unless they're a con artist or a beginner, they don't expect a functioning machine most of the time, rather they expect a lot of very difficult trial and error. Because the project is seen as one of the most difficult things, it's unfair to suspect that they're wrong based on very limited evidence. The fact is a perpetual motion machine is not ordinary physics, it's a case of something that has a special combination of properties. It's something hard to explain, not necessarily exotic energy but pretty complicated.

Someone I knew once, I think they were inspired by one of the cartoons I drew years ago, drew an analogy to 'men in black coats', 'men in grey coats', 'men in white coats', and the first category is for women.

CONTRAST MAY BE HELPFUL IN VIEWING THESE DIFFERENT ASPECTS;

(1) is like ('royalty-free dancing alien gif': Dancing Alien GIFs - Get the best GIF on GIPHY)

(2) Is like an imagine of something that looks transparent in which the sweater is invisible too.

(3) Is like: "I don't know, therefore aliens".

A meme I made myself if I remember correctly.

(4) Is like a classic experiment in basic mechanics.

THE PROBLEM WITH NEW CONSCIOUSNESS

It's argued knowing gets downgraded every generation, because each generation generates its less-and-less perfect 'picture reality' for what knowledge means. Even the vocabulary gets worse, at least since the geniuses of around 1906.

A second view is the 'first countervailing intelligence' which says there was some benefit in innocence being lost. For example, although people may not have known such big words, maybe they applied the new words to real things hopefully. So, there was a place for practical intelligence. The reality was more like practical intelligence was an excuse to do less real work. Though perhaps in an artificial kind of way they achieved something visionary. Something like being a specialist.

A third view is the 'heterodoxical intelligence' which generates a lot of energy by thinking the conventional way is wrong. It might develop new words using new laws, forgetting that a lot might have been achieved before the so-called traditionalists arrived. Some amount of history gets lost.

The fourth view is the 'second countervailing intelligence' which tries to re-assess what counts as traditional, and establish a new orthodoxy.

Then it returns to traditionalism: the new orthodoxy is partly accepted, and what people remember of the earlier traditions is treated roughly the same. This is where we are now, though we are just in the beginning stages.

Soon there will probably be another iteration of the 'first countervailing intelligence' which adopts the view that 'things always were a certain way' and that 'one way is the right way'.

Otherwise, there could be a shift of consciousness. But a shift of consciousness would probably involve a simplification to two stages, first-level orthodoxy and rebelliousness. However, if there were a simplification, it would deny the importance of new orthodoxy, and society would be thrown into a dystopia.

Thus, society depends on the second iteration of the 'first countervailing intelligence' in order to remain modern and continue. Yet what is also important is the original 'second countervailing intelligence' which gives society new things to wonder and think about. Thirdly, the original traditionalism is an actual sensibility. Fourthly, rebelliousness is what leads to the transition between periods.

—What is the purpose of knowing? (...)

Quick:

- WHAT HAPPENS WHEN YOU RECEIVE FINANCIAL ADVICE: That question often means you have just received good 'advice' but you are cursed to gain experience instead of knowing what it is. They often tell you either how to be smart but you can't, how to survive but it's difficult, or something you already know which you should apply well.
- THE TRUTH IS NEAR A famous judge often said, that one must keep the truth at arms length, but not much further. Incidentally, this is precisely how to keep truth nearby in a relativistic universe. Maybe the relative is absolute after all.
- If you want to work as a plumber or electrician, you have to go through the training, then you have to probably be better than other people doing the training at what you do, then you have to be competent and rich enough to open your own practice.
- If you want to be an artist, you will compete with millions of other

aspiring artists. You will have to have money to buy supplies, then you will have to be inspired enough to make good use of them. Finally, when you have inspiration, you will need to compete with millions of other artists not only in how inspired you are, but also how prolific you are. Even then, you will need luck, charisma, and an understanding of human psychology to even make one sale.

- If you want to use someone else's idea, even though you might not have to be genius enough to invent the idea, you still need to be genius enough to apply the idea in a genius way. In some cases a little practicality goes a lot further than simply trying to impress people.
- There was a situation where I gave someone advice about cutting up pickles to make tunafish taste better. They couldn't explains why the tunafish at work tasted so good. They thought it was the devil.
- "The ants just need to discover innovation." YY said.

What examples in your life do you see where the phrase "Don't cast your pearls before swine" applies to your choices?

Three main topics:

- Giving advice about not investing in the stock market.
- Explaining that coherence theory could be useful to an impartial scientist.
- Discussing whether perpetual motion is an original discovery.

Best Uncommon Stories / Anecdotes:

What is the most fascinating historical event from any period in your opinion?

As far as my own opinion, I think the Oct 11, 2018 confirmation of the principles of perpetual motion is fascinating.

Here we have an idea for a machine that solves all the world's practical needs, which ironically happens to be rejected by the two leading institutions of the time, science and religion...

Not only that, but the inventor, a mentally ill person living about 500 miles ftom New York, seems to have lived a pretty quiet and uneventful life leading up to the time of the discovery.

Make no mistake, it was a great discovery, as even the likes of Leonardo Da Vinci, Cornelis Drabbel, and Isaac Newton had failed to dicover it. Many thought it was a failed quest like the ancient search for the Holy Grail, the Sword Excalibur, or the Golden Fleece.

Nathan Coppedge was not a child prodigy, in fact he suffered a brain accident when he was just a baby. During his youth he yearned to become a professor like his Dad, but never developed the ability.

When in 2000, after years of simply suffering and doing homework he demonstrated a Natural Torque Device to his younger brother (who was actually a prodigy), his idea was rejected by his whole family including his brother.

Five years later, having forced himself into complete forgetfulness about the invention, he picked up courage to become an inventor for what he now thought was the first time, perhaps as a way of paying bills. However, his inventions from 2005 were failures.

In fact, apart from some mechanical shoes that turned out to be illegal to wear in public, he did no major further experimenting until he developed courage to test the basic Motive Mass Machine principle because his website featuring perpetual motion machines was receiving 60 views / day.

At this moment it seemed like no one was really interested... (except perhaps Nathan and a few other hobbyists). There was always a chance that the web traffic was random.

Nathan's first successful over-unity experiment did not occur until four years later in late 2013 (five years ago when this story was first written), when it was shown a marble could lift the same counterweight that had caused the marble to rise.

Expecting the world to start celebrating, Nathan began to think he had achieved the ultimate aim, but, meeting with silence and rejection, his experiments continued.

In May 2018 he rebuilt his Natural Torque device which he had completely forgotten about, which encouraged him to do more experiments.

Even then in May 2018 it seemed like only a handful of hobbyists recognized that special efficiencies were necessary to make perpetual motion work.

In August - October 2018 Nathan found a collaborator who replicated his earlier result, which encouraged him to get more serious.

On Oct 11, 2018 since the website Revolution Green had covered his work, he moved forward with the promising Swivel Lever Device, which he had forgotten somewhere in his notes.

This experiment and those that followed proved in effect that it was possible to create one full cycle from rest with no added energy, thereby indicating perpetual motion.

Who is the strongest camp in physics, Albert Einstein or Heisenberg?

I think it is said by physicists that they cannot say that it is not Heisenberg, but it is Einstein. When they are sure that it is Einstein, they use Heisenberg.

However, the little h stands for Planck...

What are some instances in which intellectual conceit has blinded people to simple truths that less educated people have been able to discern?

One could argue the priests were more educated, if not more intelligent, than Copernicus.

One could argue alchemiets, although they were persecuted, knew some chemistry.

One could argue the inventor of perpetual motion did not know advanced physics.

Which is your favorite anecdote about philosophers?

An artist, a scientist, and a philosopher walk into a bar.

Before taking their drink, each one is asked to explain his reasoning.

The artist replies: it has a beautiful bouquet, and drunks it up.

The scientist explains it has such-and-such molecular compound, therefore he is addicted.

The philosopher replies "What beer?" and walks out, lost in his thinking.

What is your favorite analogy?

1

Bottlemaking used to be a special talent involving sending up a kind of fluke. However, these days the world is full of bottlemakers, and people have forgotten it's not the only thing that's a big deal.

...

(That was about the contemporary imagination and perpetual motion).

...

2

Here is a dirtier one someone else originated:

An artist is to the world as a philosopher is to God:

An artist must DO the right thing, whereas a philosopher must BE the right thing.

...

(To which they say 'Get the analogy you p*******?')

What is your favorite analogy relating to science and technology?

A grasshopper is introduced to several technology fields.

Grasshopper, design a new pharmaceutical?

So he does.

Grasshopper, make a new engineering invention!

So, he does.

Then he is asked, grasshopper, give us an accurate map of deepspace.

Sorry, says grasshopper, it has fuzzy boundary conditions.

What's the difference between working in logic as a mathematician and as a philosopher?

(2019)

There's a story about this.

If you're a philosopher, you work on philosophy, then, if you're lucky you work on math.

The mathematician is already lucky.

But the philosopher is happy.

The mathematician is depressed.

But the philosopher senses beauty.

The mathematician is angry.

But the philosopher feels sensitive.

The mathematician is a know-it-all.

But the philosopher has made pretty doilies.

The mathematician is dead.

But the philosopher is a plagiarist.

The mathematician is dead.

But the philosopher learned a new word.

The mathematician is dead.

But the philosopher had a life-changing event.

They brought the mathematician back.

Now the philosopher feels dead.

Something happened to the mathematician's work.

Now the philosopher is great.

Now the mathematician is probably dead.

Now the philosopher is nothing but footnotes to Plato.

Now God is dead.

Now the only ones left are Nietzsche, Hegel, and Marx.

...

And Prof V. said, and if you look at it, it looks like a rocket. It's rocket science.

And a rocket scientist said: That's not rocket science!

And V said: It isn't? Then, what is? Pretend I have an I.Q. of 84.

And the rocket scientist said: I don't know.

And V said: There, that's what gets you. You think it's a joke, but I don't.

How is old civilization failing nowadays?

Rumor is old civilizations do not ask that question.

What's the coolest thing you ever bought?

Possibly this cup that happened to be right next to me—why?—because this cup is made with a very interesting nano-texture that feels very pleasant—pleasurable— to hold.

Not only that, but I inspired the idea for the nanotexture when I talked to someone years ago.

How different is the view on philosophy between people with science background vs humanities and arts background?

In the arts, spirituality is the ultimate goal, in science it is left far behind. A science teacher may have said this, and it was conjectured that the lower the level you think he teaches, the higher your aptitude in education.

What are some simple analogies and metaphors to help children understand the difficult times?

You can just say, "Life is imperfect sometimes. Do what you can."

A longwinded metaphor makes them think suffering is meaningful, which is bad.

What technology trends are going to be a good investment in the long run?

Here's my mysterium for the moment:

1986: Early life events inspire Nathan Coppedge (3-years-old): 1. Nathan views clothes line turnstiles at Prospect St. Development Projects (?) as beautiful machines, 2. Nathan's mother says 'they are not really machines'. 3. Nathan's friend Eileen breaks his precious green squirt gun, resulting in a feeling of unfathomable loss related to a machine. 4. Nathan's Dad's workplace features an enormous, unfeeling clunky machine the size of a building that just prints out papers, a symbol of the obsolescence of recent technology.

Shock value is hard-won. That's my tip right now. What really works is not always what you expect. Sometimes people want something good. Good, you know? Not everyone knows what it is.

When reasoning about higher dimensions, how far can analogy take us? Does it eventually become, cumbersome, unhelpful, or even misleading?

Analogy is useful in math education but not as useful in philosophy.

What was one time a kid amazed you with his knowledge?

My younger brother described a boy from my sister's birthday party we had both seen:

"He told this dirty joke, and it was seemingly brilliant at every point, and it went on and on until it seemed like two hours had passed. My conclusion is HE is a genius."

And my lesbian aunt was like "What if he's NOT a genius?"

Then what was he doing?

What is your opinion on how the world is currently...and how do you think it will be in the future?

Life is great for some people. Some great things happen which doesn't usually feel great. But life is pretty equal in some ways.

Some have fun, some live long, some have achievements, and some have money, but everyone has problems.

Rumor is if you don't have problems, watch out, the problems may come.

The guy who's life is really perfect probably dies not so long after. Like all the people that retire in California, there's something unnatural about it. They're usually gone within 15 - 20 years or even less.

The Story of the Mechanical Toy that May have Inspired Perpetual Motion

Written August 5, 2019.

One of my first encounters was with a spinning top toy, when I was extremely young, like zero to 1-year-old.

The toy was designed so that if the middle spiral rod was shoved down repeatedly, it would make a mechanical noise and begin to spin.

It was fairly large, like 8-inches across (or maybe a bit smaller than I remember). Both me and my brother played with it, and it created a sense of competitiveness and a sense that the world was full of mechanical playthings.

Why do systems thinkers say that everything is a system?

Because they are trying to find a system of everything.

Image Credit: Nathan Coppedge

The story of the psychiatric patient. If he says 'you're crazy' he's called crazy, but if he says 'we're all trees' he is considered sane. Close to the truth.

"Never go to South Africa unless you're a woman who wants to get married to a certain guy. In other words, never go to South Africa." —How can I open a research lab in South Africa for an innovative product?

"Anecdotes are about anecdotes, that is about all..." —Nathan Larkin Coppedge

I don't plan per se, I just look for better economic security, and deal as best I can with bureaucracy. (Possible quote ftom Dostoyevsky).

—How many years can you actually plan into the future?

...

I imagine creating free energy with the U.S. government might be more difficult than grasping the basic concept of wisdom in an entry-level philosophy course. However, maybe I'm wrong. —Which is easier to concentrate, knowledge or power?

...

"If someone was mature between 1991 and 2005 they could have been a millennial thinker even if they were a bit old or if they were a bit mature for a young person. If you want to be a successful business person in 2030 - 2040 though, it's probably about old money or perhaps small-scale stuff for people that were not yet mature in 2000." —Millennial and Business Ideas

"Generalism is a big opportunity in philosophy. But it could be argued philosophy is not a big opportunity. Specialization is a modest opportunity in science, if science is an opportunity. Though usually science is not the opportunity it pretends to be."

...

END

BOOK RECOMMENDATIONS

One-Page Classics

Banned Classics

The Lessons of the Master

The Story of Master Wu

All by Nathan Coppedge

Or under the pseudonym

Master Kuo

Bio

Nathan Coppedge or Nathan Larkin Coppedge (b.1982) is a philosopher, artist, inventor, poet, and member of the international honor society for philosophers. A prolific author with over 186 books published on Amazon, he is a perpetual motioneer, famous quotable, and internationally-selling Hyper-Cubist. A one-time member of Tesla Society UK online and PESWiki, and founder of many Facebook groups, he lives near Yale University.